Delaney Street Press

Never Give In!

*Inspirational Quotations for
Courageous Living*

By Criswell Freeman

DELANEY STREET PRESS
Nashville, TN 37211

ISBN 1-58334-073-4

The ideas expressed in this book are not, in all cases, exact quotations, as some have been edited for clarity and brevity. In all cases, the author has attempted to maintain the speaker's original intent. In some cases, material for this book was obtained from secondary sources, primarily print media. While every effort was made to ensure the accuracy of these sources, the accuracy cannot be guaranteed. For additions, deletions, corrections or clarifications in future editions of this text, please write DELANEY STREET PRESS.

Cover Design by Bart Dawson
Layout and Typesetting by Sue Gerdes

Printed in the United States of America
1 2 3 4 5 6 7 8 9 10 • 00 01 02 03 04

ACKNOWLEDGMENTS

The author gratefully acknowledges the helpful support of Angela Beasley Freeman, Dick and Mary Freeman, Mary Susan Freeman, Carli Freeman, Jim Gallery, and the entire team of professionals at DELANEY STREET PRESS and WALNUT GROVE PRESS.

For Bill Freeman

Table of Contents

Every noble work is at first impossible.

Thomas Carlyle

1

Never Give In!

On October 29, 1941, Winston Churchill spoke to the students and faculty at Harrow School. His four-minute speech, delivered amidst the chaos of World War II, still speaks to the hearts of courageous men and women everywhere:

"Never give in. Never give in. Never, never, never — in nothing great or small, large or petty — never give in except to conviction of honor and good sense. Never yield to force; never yield to the apparently overwhelming might of the enemy.

Do not let us speak of darker days. Let us speak rather of sterner days. These are not dark days; these are great days — the greatest days our country has ever lived, and we must all thank God that we have been allowed, each of us according to our stations, to play a part in making these days memorable in the history of our race."

Churchill's words remind us that in times of adversity, victory belongs to those who persevere. In battle as in life, the secret of success is most often summed up in two simple words: "persistence" and "courage."

Nothing in the world can take the place of persistence. Talent will not. Genius will not. Education will not. Persistence and determination alone are omnipotent.

Calvin Coolidge

If you run into a wall, don't turn around and give up. Figure out how to climb it, go through it, or work around it.
Michael Jordan

All great deeds and all great thoughts have a ridiculous beginning. Great works are often born on a street corner or in a restaurant's revolving door.
Albert Camus

You do what you can for as long as you can, and when you finally can't, you do the next best thing. You back up, but you don't give up.
Chuck Yeager

To get it right, be born with luck or else make it. Never give up. Get the knack of getting people to help you and also pitch in yourself.

Ruth Gordon

Never give up. Keep your thoughts and your mind always on the goal.

Tom Bradley

If I had permitted my failures to discourage me, I cannot see any way in which I would ever have made progress.

Calvin Coolidge

Don't give up
at halftime. Concentrate
on winning the
second half.

Bear Bryant

Never give up and never give in.
Hubert H. Humphrey

If I had to cram all my tournament experience into one sentence, I would say, "Don't give up and don't let up!"
Tony Lema

To endure is the first thing that a child ought to learn, and it is the thing which he will have the most need to know.
Jean Jacques Rousseau

When you get into a tight place and everything goes against you, till it seems as though you could not hang on a minute longer, never give up then, for that is just the place and time that the tide will turn.

Harriet Beecher Stowe

Never go backward.
Attempt, and do it with all your might.
Determination is power.

Charles Simmons

Diligence overcomes difficulties;
    sloth makes them.
                    Ben Franklin

Failure is the path of least persistence.
                    Old-Time Saying

There is no chance, no destiny, no fate
    that can hinder or control the firm
    resolve of a determined soul.
                    Ella Wheeler Wilcox

A wise man will make more
   opportunities than he finds.
                              Francis Bacon

Perhaps perseverance has been
   the radical principle of every
   truly great character.
                              John Foster

Patience and diligence, like faith,
   move mountains.
                              William Penn

Fight the good fight with all thy might.
William Tecumseh Sherman

I have not yet begun to fight.
John Paul Jones

What counts is not the size of the dog
in the fight, but the size of the fight
in the dog.
Dwight D. Eisenhower

2

Adversity

In difficult times, we learn lessons that we could have learned in no other way. We learn about life, but, more importantly, we learn about ourselves.

Adversity visits everyone — no human being is beyond Old Man Trouble's reach. But Old Man Trouble is not only an unwelcomed guest, he is also an invaluable teacher. If we are to become mature human beings, it is our duty to learn from the inevitable hardships and heartbreaks of life. Here's how.

He knows not his own strength
who has not met adversity.
Ben Johnson

We cannot learn without pain.
Aristotle

There is no education like adversity.
Benjamin Disraeli

Difficulty, my brethren, is the nurse
of greatness — a harsh nurse,
who roughly rocks her foster-children
into strength and athletic proportion.
William C. Bryant

Great crises produce great men and
great deeds of courage.
John F. Kennedy

Difficulties is the name given to things
that it is our business to overcome.
Ernest J. King

There is no success without hardship.
Sophocles

I have always grown from
my problems and challenges,
from the things that didn't work out.
That's when I've really learned.
Carol Burnett

Adversity reveals genius,
prosperity conceals it.

Horace

That which does
not kill me makes
me stronger.

Nietzsche

Don't be disquieted in times of adversity. Be firm with dignity and self-reliant with vigor.

Chiang Kai-Shek

A man of character finds a special attractiveness in difficulty, since it is only by coming to grips with difficulty that he can realize his potentialities.

Charles de Gaulle

The good things of prosperity are to be wished; but the good things that belong to adversity are to be admired.

Seneca

Adversity is the state
in which a man
most easily becomes
acquainted with
himself.

Samuel Johnson

It is the character of a brave and resolute
man not to be ruffled by adversity
and not to desert his post.

Cicero

As threshing separates the wheat from
the chaff, so does affliction purify virtue.

Richard Francis Burton

Adversity has the effect of eliciting
talents which in prosperous circumstances
would have lain dormant.

Horace

It takes as much courage to have tried
and failed as it does to have tried
and succeeded.
Anne Morrow Lindbergh

Difficulties are meant to rouse,
not discourage. The human spirit
is to grow strong by conflict.
William E. Channing

The greatest test of courage on earth is
to bear defeat without losing heart.
Robert G. Ingersoll

Sweet are the uses of adversity.
Shakespeare

Fire is the test of gold;
adversity is the test of strong men.
Seneca

If you can't stand the heat,
get out of the kitchen.
Harry Truman

3

Courage

Running away from problems only perpetuates them. As Shakespeare correctly observed, "Cowards die many times before their deaths; the valiant never taste of death but once."

Fear begets more fear. Anxiety is a poor counselor. Worry leads to emotional paralysis. But when we take a straightforward approach to our problems and tackle them with courage and determination, miracles happen.

Difficult times call for courageous measures. The words on the following pages remind us that victory does indeed belong to the bold. So if you're facing a difficult situation, do the courageous thing. Courage has a way of overcoming adversity. Always has — always will.

Courage and perseverance have a magical talisman, before which difficulties disappear and obstacles vanish into thin air.
John Quincy Adams

Courage is the price that life exacts for granting peace. The soul that knows it not, knows no release from little things.
Amelia Earhart

We must have courage to be happy.
Henri Frédéric Amiel

True miracles are created by men when they use the courage and intelligence that God gave them.

Jean Anouilh

All happiness depends upon
courage and work.
Honoré de Balzac

Whether you are a man or woman,
you will never do anything in this world
without courage. It is the greatest
quality of the mind next to honor.
James Allen

Fear brings out the worst in everybody.
Maya Angelou

Courage is fear that has said its prayers.
Dorothy Bernard

Courage is always the surest wisdom.
Winston Churchill

Fear is an illusion.

Michael Jordan

Facing it — always facing it — that's the way to get through.

Joseph Conrad

Courage is doing what you're afraid
to do. There can be no courage unless
you're scared.
Edward Rickenbacker

Courage is being scared to death —
and saddling up anyway.
John Wayne

Do what you fear and the death of fear
is certain.
Ralph Waldo Emerson

Courage is its own reward.

Plautus

Courage is a special kind of knowledge:
the knowledge of how to fear what
ought to be feared and how not to fear
what ought not to be feared.

David Ben-Gurion

It is the perpetual dread of fear, the fear
of fear, that shapes the face
of a brave man.

Georges Bernanos

The first and great commandment is don't let them scare you.

Elmer Davis

Courage is the first of human qualities
because it is the quality which
guarantees all the others.

Winston Churchill

Without courage,
wisdom bears no fruit.

Baltasar Gracián

Courage is a kind of salvation.

Plato

Become so wrapped up in something
that you forget to be afraid.
Lady Bird Johnson

You gain strength, courage,
and confidence every time
you look fear in the face.
Eleanor Roosevelt

The great part of courage is having done
a thing before.
Ralph Waldo Emerson

Courage is the virtue which champions
the cause of the right.

Cicero

True courage is not the brutal force
of vulgar heroes, but the firm resolve
of virtue and reason.

Alfred North Whitehead

God grant me the courage not to give
up what I think is right, even if I think
it is hopeless.

Chester Nimitz

One man with courage
is a majority.

Andrew Jackson

Success is never final.
Failure is never fatal.
Courage is the
only thing.

Winston Churchill

Do not borrow trouble
by dreading tomorrow.
It is the dark menace
of the future that makes
cowards of us all.

Dorothy Dix

What you can do
or dream you can do,
begin it. Boldness has
genius, power, and
magic in it.

Goethe

He who finds Fortune on his side
should go briskly ahead, for she is
wont to favor the bold.
Baltasar Gracián

We learn courage by going forward
whenever fear urges us back.
David Seabury

We cannot solve problems except
by solving them.
M. Scott Peck

Courage is grace under pressure.
Ernest Hemingway

Anger is a prelude to courage.
Eric Hoffer

Pain nourishes courage. You can't be
brave if you've only had wonderful
things happen to you.
Mary Tyler Moore

Courage conquers all things.

Ovid

Despair is an evil counselor.

Sir Walter Scott

Live from miracle to miracle.

Artur Rubinstein

The greatest test of courage on earth
is to bear defeat without losing heart.
Robert G. Ingersoll

Courage is the basic virtue for everyone
so long as he continues to grow,
to move ahead.
Rollo May

In adversity, a man is saved by hope.
Menander

Nothing is as valuable to a man
as courage.

Terence

Fortune favors the brave.

Terence

To have courage for whatever comes
in life — everything lies in that.
Saint Teresa of Avila

Fear corrupts.

John Steinbeck

Keep your fears to yourself,
but share your courage
with others.
Robert Louis Stevenson

When you get to the end of your rope,
tie a knot and hang on.
Franklin D. Roosevelt

4

Work

Elbert Hubbard observed, "When troubles arise, wise men go to their work." Easier said than done. During difficult times, we are tempted to complain, to worry, to blame, and to do very little else. Usually, complaints and worries change nothing. Intelligent work, on the other hand, changes everything.

Whatever the problem, hard work — if it's thoughtfully planned and carefully executed — will help. So the next time *you* feel the urge to gripe or fret, go to your work. Work beats worry every time.

If the power to do hard
work is not talent,
it is the best possible
substitute for it.

James A. Garfield

It is the first of all problems for a man
to find out what kind of work he is
to do in this universe.
Thomas Carlyle

The one predominant duty is to find
one's work and do it.
Charlotte Perkins Gilman

No man is born whose work is not born
with him. There is always work, and tools
to work with, for those who will.
James Russell Lowell

Diligence makes good luck.
Ben Franklin

Begin — to begin is half the work.
Ausonius

I realized that with hard work, the world
was your oyster. You could do anything
you wanted to do. I learned that
at a young age.
Chris Evert Lloyd

Be like a postage stamp: Stick to one thing till you get there.

Josh Billings

It is easier to do a job
right than to explain
why you didn't.

Martin Van Buren

Each man's talent is his call.
There is one direction in which
all doors are open to him.
Ralph Waldo Emerson

Think enthusiastically about everything,
especially your work.
Norman Vincent Peale

Do your work with your whole heart,
and you will succeed — there is
so little competition.
Elbert Hubbard

The more I want to get something done,
the less I call it work.

Richard Bach

Nothing is really work unless you would
rather be doing something else.

James Matthew Barrie

Like what you do. If you don't like it,
do something else.

Paul Harvey

Luck? I don't know anything about luck. I've never banked on it and I'm afraid of people who do. Luck to me is something else: Hard work — and realizing what is opportunity and what isn't.

Lucille Ball

I've always believed that if you put in the work, the results will come.

Michael Jordan

If my life had been made up of eight-hour days, I do not believe I could have accomplished a great deal.

Thomas Edison

Talent is only a starting point in
this business. You've got to keep on
working that talent.

Irving Berlin

Inspiration comes from
working every day.

Charles Baudelaire

Talent alone won't make you a success.
Neither will being in the right place at
the right time, unless you are ready.
The most important question is:
"Are your ready?"

Johnny Carson

No great thing is created suddenly.

Epictetus

If I do my full duty, the rest
will take care of itself.
George S. Patton

The reward of a thing well done
is to have done it.
Ralph Waldo Emerson

Duty is ours; consequences are God's.
Stonewall Jackson

Believe in the Lord
and He will do half
the work — the
last half.

Cyrus Curtis

Work for your soul's sake.

Edgar Lee Masters

5

Faith

G. K. Chesterton writes, "There is one thing which gives radiance to everything. It is the idea of something around the corner." But during times of adversity, that "something around the corner" may provoke more fear than hope. When fear looms large, a profound but simple antidote is required: faith.

If you are approaching a crossroads, approach it optimistically. And if you need a surefire prescription for "turning the corner," consider the quotations that follow.

Honor begets honor.
Trust begets trust.
Faith begets faith.
And hope is the
mainspring
of life.

Henry Lewis Stimson

One of the things I learned the hard way was that it doesn't pay to get discouraged. Keeping busy and making optimism a way of life can restore your faith in yourself.

Lucille Ball

To persevere, trusting in what hopes he has, is courage in a man.

Euripides

We have a right to believe that faith is the stronger emotion because it is positive whereas fear is negative.

John Paul Jones

Seeds of faith are always within us;
sometimes it takes a crisis to nourish
and encourage their growth.
Susan L. Taylor

Faith begins where Reason
sinks exhausted.
Albert Pike

In actual life, every great enterprise
begins with and takes its first
forward step through faith.
Friedrich von Schlegel

Keep your face to the sunshine and
you cannot see the shadows.
Helen Keller

Perpetual optimism is a force multiplier.
Colin Powell

If you think you can win, you can win.
Faith is necessary to victory.
William Hazlitt

Faith is the antiseptic of the soul.

Walt Whitman

Faith is an activity. It is something
that has to be applied.
Corrie ten Boom

Faith can put a candle
in the darkest night.
Margaret Sangster

Faith is not believing that God can,
but that God will!
Abraham Lincoln

Alas! The fearful unbelief is unbelief
in yourself.

Thomas Carlyle

Begin to weave and God will provide
the thread.

German Proverb

Nothing is impossible to a willing heart.

John Heywood

Great hopes make great men.
Thomas Fuller

Never take away hope from any man.
Oliver Wendell Holmes, Sr.

In adversity, a man is saved by hope.
Menander

Worry and anxiety
are sand in the
machinery of life;
faith is the oil.

E. Stanley Jones

6

Goals

Lewis Carroll wrote, "If you don't know where you are going, any road will get you there." Mr. Carroll might have added that many of those roads are dead ends.

Since all of us possess a limited number of days in which to travel the highways of life, we are wise to plan our journeys carefully. We do so by setting clear, definable goals.

Efforts and courage
are not enough without
purpose and direction.

John F. Kennedy

Goals help you overcome
short-term problems.
Hannah More

A good goal is like a strenuous exercise:
It makes you stretch.
Mary Kay Ash

Great minds have purposes;
others have wishes.
Washington Irving

Follow your desire as long as you live;
we should not lessen the time of following
desire, for the wasting of time is
an abomination to the spirit.

Ptahhotep

If you want to accomplish the goals
of your life, you have to begin
with the Spirit.

Oprah Winfrey

Make a success of living by seeing
the goal and aiming for it unswervingly.

Cecil B. De Mille

If you're climbing the ladder of life, go rung by rung, step by step, and don't look too far up. Set your goals high, but take one step at a time.

Donny Osmond

Pursue one great decisive aim with force and determination.

Karl von Clausewitz

Hold yourself responsible for a higher standard than anyone else expects of you. Never excuse yourself.

Henry Ward Beecher

Make no little plans;
they have no magic
to stir the blood.

Daniel H. Burnham

Great things are done when man and
mountain meet.
William Blake

It's not the mountain we conquer,
but ourselves.
Edmund Hillary

Nothing will come of nothing.
Dare mighty things.
Shakespeare

Enthusiasm for one's goal lessens the disagreeableness of working toward it.
Thomas Eakins

My interest is in the future because
I am going to spend the rest
of my life there.
Charles F. Kettering

Where we stand is not as important
as the direction in which
we are moving.
Oliver Wendell Holmes, Jr

A good plan executed now is better than a perfect plan executed next week.

George S. Patton

In the long run we only hit what we
aim at. Aim high.
Henry David Thoreau

We aim above the mark to hit the mark.
Every act has some falsehood
or exaggeration in it.
Ralph Waldo Emerson

If you would hit the mark, you must aim
a little above it.
Henry Wadsworth Longfellow

The ultimate function
of prophecy is not
to tell the future but
to make it.

W. W. Wagar

I like dreams of the future better
than the history of the past.
Thomas Jefferson

The plans of the diligent lead to profit.
Proverbs 21:5

Nothing great was ever achieved
without enthusiasm.
Ralph Waldo Emerson

The best way to make
your dreams come true
is to wake up.

Paul Valery

Whatever course you have chosen for
yourself, it will not be a chore but an
adventure if you bring to it a sense of the
glory of striving, if your sights are set far
above the merely secure and mediocre.
David Sarnoff

Not failure, but low aim, is the crime.
James Russell Lowell

You don't have to be a fantastic hero
to do certain things — to compete. You
can be just an ordinary chap, sufficiently
motivated to reach challenging goals.
Edmund Hillary

When you reach for the stars you may not make it, but you won't come up with a handful of mud, either.

Leo Burnett

If you would create something, you must be something.

Goethe

First say to yourself what you would be; then do what you have to do.

Epictetus

Arriving at one goal is the starting
point of another.

John Dewey

Never run out of goals.

Earl Nightingale

Always leave something to wish for;
otherwise you will be miserable from
your very happiness.

Baltasar Gracián

Without some goal and some effort
to reach it, no man can live.
Fyodor Dostoyevsky

Hell is to drift; heaven is to steer.
George Bernard Shaw

The tragedy of life doesn't lie in not
reaching your goal. The tragedy lies
in having no goal to reach.
Benjamin E. Mays

Decide exactly what you want in life,
write it down in detail, and decide that
you will pay the price to achieve it.
Brian Tracy

A goal is a dream with a deadline.
Harvey Mackay

Begin with an intense burning desire
for something definite.
Napoleon Hill

Nobody ever drew up his plans for life
so well but what the facts and the years
and experience always introduce
some modification.

Terence

It is a bad plan that admits
no modification.

Publilius Syrus

The method of the enterprising is to
plan with audacity and
execute with vigor.

Christian Bovee

Admire those who
attempt great things,
even if they fail.

Seneca

7

Opportunity

Ralph Waldo Emerson writes, "The world is all gates, all opportunities, strings of tension waiting to be struck."

All of us are surrounded by a swirl of great opportunities, but often we're so wrapped up in the daily grind that we fail to notice. So we continue to do what we've always done, wondering why we get what we've always gotten.

If you're tired of the same old results, open your eyes to the opportunities that surround you. Make big plans; dream big dreams; and then get to work. Because big dreams do come true, but not until you dream them — and reach for them.

There is no security
on this earth; there
is only opportunity.
General Douglas MacArthur

Every man is free to rise as far as he's
able or willing, but the degree to which
he thinks determines the degree
to which he'll rise.

Ayn Rand

Take the obvious, add a cupful of brains,
a generous pinch of imagination,
a bucketful of courage and daring,
stir well and bring to a boil.

Bernard Baruch

Do it big or stay in bed.

Larry Kelly

Real miracles are created by men when
they use their God-given courage
and intelligence.

Jean Anouilh

Learning is the discovery that
something is possible.

Fritz Perls

The only thing that stands between
a man and what he wants from life is
often merely the will to try it and the
faith to believe that it is possible.

Rich DeVos

Think big. Act big.
Dream big.

Conrad Hilton

No great man ever complained about
lack of opportunity.
Ralph Waldo Emerson

Nothing is so often irretrievably missed
as a daily opportunity.
Marie von Ebner-Eschenbach

The opportunity that God sends
does not wake up him who is asleep.
Senegalese Proverb

Opportunities multiply as they are seized; they die when neglected. Life is a long line of opportunities.
John Wicker

Great things are not something accidental but must certainly be willed.
Vincent van Gogh

The successful person is the one who had a chance and took it.
Roger Babson

As soon as you trust yourself, you will know how to live.

Goethe

Don't be afraid to take a big step
if one is indicated. You can't cross
a chasm in two small jumps.
David Lloyd-George

Opportunity is missed because
it is dressed in overalls and
looks like work.
Thomas Edison

I have learned to use the word "impossible"
with the greatest caution.
Wernher von Braun

Impossibility is a word only to be found
in the dictionary of fools.
Napoleon I

Ask yourself this question:
"How big can I dream?"
Conrad Hilton

8

Life

When Winston Churchill advised, "Never give in," he might well have added that never giving *in* means never giving *up* on life. During good times and bad, life should be viewed as a precious gift and a splendid experiment. As Helen Keller observed, "Life is either a daring adventure or nothing." May yours be a grand and glorious adventure.

Begin at once to live
and count each day
a separate life.

Seneca

Life is a journey, not a
destination. Happiness
is not "there," but here,
not tomorrow,
but today.

Sidney Greenberg

A man is never old until regrets take
the place of his dreams.

John Barrymore

No matter how long you live,
die young.

Elbert Hubbard

Whether it's the best of times
or the worst of times, it's the only time
you've got.

Art Buchwald

Life is in the living, in the tissue
of every day and hour.
Stephen Leacock

Live with no time out.
Simone de Beauvoir

Plunge boldly into the thick of life!
Goethe

Do you love life? Then do not squander time, for that's the stuff life is made of.

Ben Franklin

The passing minute is every man's equal possession.

Marcus Aurelius

Nobody's gonna live for you.

Dolly Parton

We find in life exactly what we
put into it.
Ralph Waldo Emerson

Life is what we make it.
Always has been. Always will be.
Grandma Moses

Live out your life in its full meaning.
It is God's life.
Josiah Royce

The greatest use of a life is to spend it for something that will outlast it.
William James

Assume responsibility for the quality of your own life.
Norman Cousins

Nothing in life is to be feared. It is only to be understood.
Marie Curie

My recipe for life is not being afraid
of myself.
Eartha Kitt

The tragedy of life is not so much what
men suffer as what they miss.
Thomas Carlyle

When life kicks you, let it kick you
forward.
E. Stanley Jones

Make your life a mission —
not an intermission.
Arnold Glasgow

Find the journey's end in every step.
Ralph Waldo Emerson

It is not enough to reach for
the brass ring. You must also enjoy
the merry-go-round.
Julie Andrews

God, give us the serenity to accept what cannot be changed; Give us courage to change what should be changed; Give us the wisdom to distinguish one from the other.

Reinhold Niebuhr

Don't take life
too seriously...
you'll never
get out of it
alive.

Elbert Hubbard

Sources

About the Author

Criswell Freeman is a Doctor of Clinical Psychology living in Nashville, Tennessee. In addition to this text, Dr. Freeman is also the author of many other titles including his bestselling self help book *When Life Throws You a Curveball, Hit It*.

About
DELANEY STREET PRESS

DELANEY STREET PRESS publishes books designed to inspire and entertain readers of all ages. DELANEY STREET books are distributed by WALNUT GROVE PRESS. For more information, call 1-800-256-8584.